23 Ways to Fail an (Agile) Transformation.

The Ultimate Guide to Eliminating Self-Organization and Employee Motivation

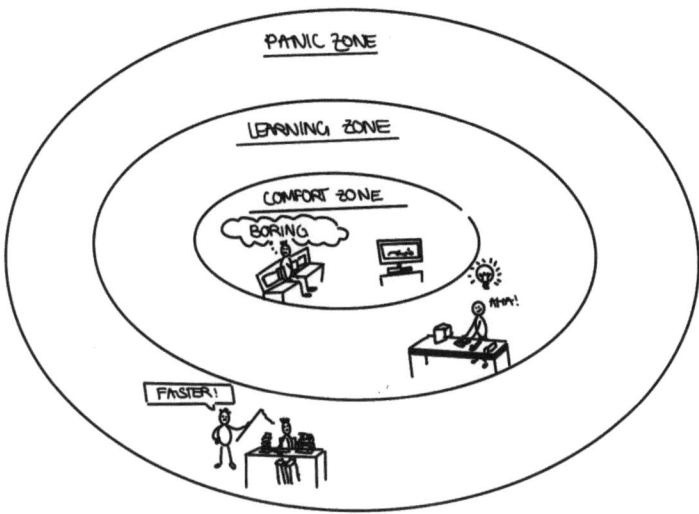

Laura & ST have been supporting individuals, teams and companies in (agile) change projects for many years. Sometimes this has been very disappointing and frustrating. As a self-therapeutic measure, they began to write short messages in which they satirized or simply quoted their environment. Comments like: "You can do that any way you like, but not like that" or "Testing? We don't do that, it's far too expensive. We implement changes live" or "This is a very good method, but unfortunately it doesn't work for us" or "In the time planning takes, I can also work on something for real" brightened the depressed mood. In the course of time, small drawings were added and the idea for this book was born. To make sure the content is not only negatively connotated, they have described improvement suggestions with each anti-tip.

23 Ways to Fail an (Agile) Transformation.

The Ultimate Guide to Eliminating
Self-Organization and Employee Motivation

#teamagile GbR
Laura Sophie Aichroth & ST Kambor-Wiesenberg

Bibliographic information of the Deutsche Nationalbibliothek: The Deutsche Nationalbibliothek lists this publication in the Deutsche Nationalbibliografie; detailed bibliographic data can be found on the Internet at https://portal.dnb.de/.

Cover design, typesetting and illustrations: #teamagile GbR. Production and publishing: BoD - Books on Demand, Norderstedt.

Translation by Katharina Louise Aichroth.

The original edition was published in 2019 under the German title: 23 Wege um eine (agile) Transformation an die Wand zu fahren.

1st edition 2020, ISBN: 9783752620160

Laura Sophie Aichroth, M. Sc.

The development of human beings - as individuals and in the system - has always been at the center of Laura's interest. With her background in business and organizational psychology, it is her goal to bring teams and organizations to fulfilling collaboration and value creation - in start-ups, medium-sized and large organizations at home and abroad. In her more than ten years of professional experience, she has inspired and supported individuals and teams to further develop ways of thinking and processes with tools and methods, from know-how to know-why. There are no off-the-shelf solutions, because depending on the context, it is necessary to make use of New Work approaches from the toolbox and to develop suitable solutions. She has worked with IT and non-IT teams.

Contact: laura@teamagile.org

ST Kambor-Wiesenberg, Graduate computer scientist & MBA

A bouquet of experience helps in dealing calmly with new situations and challenges. ST moves with ease between the disciplines: He is a trained electronics engineer, computer scientist and physicist, MBA and visual artist. A cross-functional team packed into one individual between craft, technology, culture, society, art and economy. He brings openness, communication skills and a mentality for working with cross-functional teams and helps to build bridges. As an agile coach, he is passionate about getting people and teams to perform at their best on their own initiative. He succeeds in doing this across borders, having already worked in Europe, Asia, the USA and various regions of Germany.

Contact: st@teamagile.org

Contents

Prologue

Everything has been said and written down and yet we still have the impression that agile, self-organized collaboration is hardly to be found in companies in a functioning, value-creating, fulfilling way. A lot of people are tired of the word "agile" and are already longing for the next trend or waiting for this trend to pass. Why is it that hard?

The aim of this book is to share pitfalls and effective ways out. We have come up with an amazing number of scenarios in a short period of time - we will start with 23. We publish these and possibly other ways to agile failure on our website www.teamagile.org and on various social networks. The hashtag is #agilewaystofail. By the way, you can do that, too. This book is licensed under a Creative Commons Attribution - Non Commercial 4.0 International License. This means that as long as you mention our name and the license, you can copy and distribute the material in any format or medium. You can remix, modify, and build on it for any non-commercial purpose. Have fun with it!

The book can be seen as a self-therapeutic measure of two agile coaches and organizational developers who have a great passion for people, cooperation and self-organization. In different projects we have noticed the same patterns again and again. To better cope with these ourselves, we have started to write down and draw what we have to do to kill self-organization, motivation and agility. In this book we describe scenarios, beliefs and often heard or experienced behaviors that show exactly what agility or self-organization don't mean. Everybody can complain; therefore, we describe concrete steps, assistance and recommendations for change in these situations from our experience. We have divided the book into five sections and assigned chapters to these sections. The areas are Management and General Demotivation, Human Resources and Attitude, Software Developers and IT, Agile Washing and Product Development and Customer Contact. However, the content is often transferable to other areas as well.

We have worked with different frameworks, national and international teams, in German or English, in different company sizes at home and abroad - from start-ups to corporations. Our experience is manifold, from a Scrum Master activity to an agile coach, the introduction of agile work with training of the participants (Scrum Master, Product Owner, Agile Coach, Agile Leader) up to the accompaniment and responsibility of (digital) transformations in the area of organizational development. We accompany teams and companies with regard to product, team and technology. We both have different certifications and have worked with software development teams in various companies according to Scrum and Kanban for several years - with the accompaniment of the ceremonies (Review, Retro, Planning, Refinement, Daily), team development, administration of the toolchain for digital mapping of cooperation and improvement of processes.

CHAPTER 1

Management and General Demotivation

A company could be such a great thing if only it didn't have those annoying employees. Simply throwing out uncomfortable colleagues is no longer up to date, it tends to go down badly on social networks. But there is one way to separate the wheat from the chaff, the 4V method® (derived from the German words: Verunsichern, Verärgern, Vergraulen): unsettle, waste, annoy, drive away. Either the employees stay and become part of the system or they leave voluntarily.

Don't practice what you preach!

What applies to general employees does not necessarily apply to managers. Being late for a meeting? Having the assistant book private holidays? Answering e-mails during a meeting? Cutting in line at the cafeteria? Exclusive parking spaces? No problem at all. You are important and your time is more valuable than that of others.

It sounds simple and in theory (hopefully) everyone agrees that you should practice the kind of behavior you preach to your fellow human beings, employees and colleagues. Nevertheless, people like to fall back into old habits and allow themselves the right to behave in a way that would bother them in others - telling themselves they have a valid justification for their behavior.

If you are able to implement decisions, make sure that visibly different classes in companies (e.g. separate canteen for the management, parking spaces for executives or senior management, different equipment than that for the "average" employee, etc.) are abolished. You can start by not using these perks. Only when you yourself feel the pain of impractical or even obstructive infrastructure you will understand the problem and be motivated to implement changes and be serious about carrying them forward. People with "power" should use the same things as people without power, e.g. restrooms, technology, IT infrastructure, office equipment or parking lots.

A negative example for this is a customer where management had roofed parking spaces in front of their offices. There were too few parking spaces for the remaining employees. Instead of thinking about a usable concept, parking attendants were asked to stick notes on cars that had not been parked in accordance with the regulations and the cars would be towed away by towing companies in the event of a repeat. Their proposed solution: indicating an alternate parking space 20 minutes away. There was no parking problem for the management. No matter whether it was raining, snowing or scorching hot - their cars stood covered and dry right in front of the door. They didn't care that 30% of their staff were already fed up with the company by the time they walked through the entrance door. Especially as a modern company, technical solutions would be appropriate here: parking guidance systems, parking lot occupancy displays via app or mobile website, Segways, electric scooters or electric golf carts to get to the alternate parking lot, loan umbrellas, a token system that employees could park x times a month in front parking lots if something has to be transported, or they have specific plans - the tokens could be exchanged so that employees using public transport or bicycles have advantages - just to name a few.

Avoiding a discrepancy between practicing and preaching begins with a few simple but very effective steps that require no rocket science, but only discipline and will. And the good thing is that you can start immediately and improvement is just one decision away:

1. Be punctual - Plan appointments in your calendar and make them end five before and begin five after, so that you are prepared in any case, can prepare yourself mentally for the next appointment, arrive on time and have already fetched a coffee.

2. Always come prepared for appointments - Block times in your calendar to prepare for appointments and always invite to appointments with goal and agenda. We stubbornly ask for goals and agendas for all appointments, help shaping them and clarifying in advance what should be worked on or discussed in the appointment. In case of doubt, we consistently cancel appointments without goals and agenda if the inviting parties don't want goals and an agenda.

3. Document properly. Knowledge is power - That is a religious but very common doctrine. People in organizations get sick, go on vacation or change jobs. Document for yourself and others to a degree that the work could continue without you. Allow others to find information in familiar, unambiguous places without having to ask you. You will find that it will save you a lot of time and nerves if those who are interested can meet their - somewhat overworked term - debt to be collected (in German Holschuld).

4. Stick to time boxes - Decisions that are not made within 55 minutes will not be made in 65 minutes. Always keep an eye on the time for a task or appointment and actively drive decisions and the agenda forward, even if you don't lead the appointment. Once the goal has been achieved and the agenda has been completed, everyone is happy to have time left and to devote

themselves to new tasks. If there is not enough time to reach the planned goal, arrange a follow-up appointment. It is important to take an active part and to notice in time when there is not enough time. If 50 minutes and 10 agenda items are planned for the meeting and point 2 is still being discussed after 30 minutes, something has to be changed, e.g. five minutes of discussion per item. If there is no decision on the point, it must be decided whether to adjourn this point or another.

5. Be focused - On all tasks. Don't eat, turn off your smartphone /mute it, put away anything that might distract you. We humans are not made for simultaneous activities. We are better if we concentrate on one task, complete it and tackle the next. Interruptions always result in the sum of the individual attempts to complete a task taking longer than to complete the task in one go. Furthermore, the probability of errors increases. It's better to take more conscious breaks and then focus again.

6. Be honest - In lectures, at trade fairs, at recruiting events or in marketing campaigns. Not telling the truth is just a very expensive loan with uncertain side effects. If you have lost the trust of your employees, it is very difficult to get it back. And what applies to your employees also applies to customers. Don't promise anything that doesn't exist (yet). Even if you don't tell an untruth directly, but only give the impression of something that doesn't correspond to the truth, this will eventually lead to disappointed expectations.

Make it harder to spend money!

Build slow, expensive and above all non-transparent processes as the only procurement option for your workforce. If the purchasing process is as complicated as possible, employees will think twice whether they need something or not. This way you can save money!

Employees build houses in their private lives, have children and take responsibility for investments. In the context of their employee existence, they are often not even expected to be able to decide when they need tools, office supplies or further training for their work. Create clear, simple processes and give your employees responsibility. Figuratively speaking, the sport, the playing field and the rules must be known to everyone in order to determine very clearly when there is a warning, a yellow card and a red card. It is extremely helpful to settle the following points for everyone:

- Transparent cost centers and budgets (easiest per team) for office supplies, software licenses, etc.
- Clear criteria for the use of further training with the agreement

to pass on the acquired knowledge to other colleagues. Define the format of transferring the knowledge before the booking of the training. Then the conditions are transparent for everyone.

- Processes that are accessible to everyone. If a central procurement has been placed, the person placing the order must be able to see its status at any time. This avoids frequent enquiries. Modern, transparent IT systems relieve the workload on purchasing employees and also on employees in the departments, who always know the status of their orders.

- Many employees find it valuable to be able to choose their own work equipment. Imagine you have to spend all day working with a tool you don't like.

We once had a conversation with a person who had a company car with a driver, and came to talk about this topic. Usually, the person being driven chooses the vehicle. She thought it was very strange because the driver has to drive the whole day and therefore, he should be able to choose the vehicle. In addition, the driver had been driving for many years and had a lot of experience, he was the expert. She liked brand X better (which she didn't tell the driver, otherwise he would have felt obliged to choose brand X), but the driver chose brand Y, so she was driven in a car by brand Y. This is a good example of how to delegate decisions to the most capable person to make a decision.

Obstruct changes!

Always answer critical questions with "We've always done it this way" or "It's worked." Alternatively: "Basically a good idea, but it wouldn't work for us". If everything stays the way it is, it secures your right to exist. Changes could lead to a deterioration of your situation.

Above all, new colleagues bring a fresh view on working methods, processes and habits. If we spend some time with a company, do a job for some time or work in a certain constellation for a longer period of time, we become operationally blind. Let new employees i.e. improve the onboarding process or act as mentors for next new colleagues to make sure their successors don't have to experience the same struggles they had to experience. Complaining is always easier than actually changing something. Be open to constructive criticism and give up responsibility so that employees realize that they have room to maneuver.

- Regular, joint, structured reviews of time periods and themes help to identify and determine what needs to be improved. Retrospectives are a popular format to collect what went well and what went badly, and then to agree who will do what by when to remedy these shortcomings.

- Install a platform (pinboard or digital solution) to collect new ideas and work with the team to determine which ones will be implemented. Of course, this can also be greatly inflated under fancy names like innovation management. Or you and your team can simply start thinking about how you can record changes and change needs and decide on concrete measures.

We all have to deal with change because the world around us is dynamic. If nothing has changed in your work, processes and/or environment for a very long time, this is not a good sign. This may feel safe and comfortable for some time, but there will be no growth in the comfort zone - in many dimensions such as personality or knowledge and ability - but rather the opposite. That is why it is important to regularly put yourself in the learning zone in order to facilitate further development. The innermost area is the comfort zone, the second the learning zone and the third the panic zone (see p. 1). In both, the comfort zone and in the panic zone, you reduce in different dimensions. Being in the panic zone makes you feel bad faster than being in the comfort zone. It is important to always know which zone you are in. It is important to notice this in yourself and in others and to take it into account as you learn.

Self-organization means: you say it, the others do it!

Preach self-organization and then manage individuals, or you'll abolish your position. Don't worry about the environment.

First of all, make yourself aware why you want self-organization and whether you really want it and can endure it. While classically hierarchically structured organizations are all about managing individuals, working with self-organized teams is exclusively about creating an environment in which the teams can work trouble-free and focus purely on the core business. What does that mean?

- Hold back consistently with your content-related, technical opinion. The principle of the invisible gun is applied here and means that your disciplinary or hierarchically subordinate team is inclined to adopt your opinion. However, the team consists of experts on the one hand and on the other hand of people who are responsible for the implementation of the decision and will live with it, because they are confronted with the consequences in their daily work.

- Do not comment on ideas and decisions with a "good" or "I like that". Just evaluate the results. Every statement influences the team.

- Work purely on a result-oriented level, supported by indicators. Describe your expectations of the result before the team starts its work and let the team decide on the way to go. Did you expect the result to be different or did you mean something different? If the result is different than what you expected, you have formulated your expectations inadequately. However, if all the acceptance criteria you mentioned earlier are met, learn from them and next time take more time to formulate your functional expectations for the result. A ping pong for results is very frustrating for the team, slows you down and is expensive (time invested, lost sales, waste of resources etc.).

Better not do anything!

Avoid doing as many things someone might misunderstand as possible. "It's always better to not do anything than to make a mistake" must become an important motto. Avoid confrontation and resentment. The more inconspicuous you are, the fewer risks you run. Problems that come on their own go away on their own.

The word error culture is often used and everyone is talking about a cultural change to be striven for, especially in the context of transformations. In this context, culture is nothing more than lived behavior in connection with the experience gained. Culture cannot be bought and cannot be copied. In our experience, a cultural change is often widely announced, initiated or simply decided upon in companies. Mostly, nothing happens, at most employees' frustration gets combined with a growing lack of credibility and dwindling trust in management. Other times, negative experiences are made when employees actually take the invitation to change their behavior seriously.

In the systems of our society, such as kindergarten, school, university and companies, we have learned over many years not to make mistakes, as this leads to sanctions. Freedom from mistakes leads to recognition and progress. Fear arises. This fear coupled with a need for recognition and connection is a driver in professional behavior for most people. Mistakes, problems and disputes are negatively connotated terms that should be avoided. This creates a culture that prevents progress. The motto: Rather than making a mistake or bringing unpleasant problems to light, I prefer to do nothing at all. Logical enough, but what now?

Initiate new rituals to share the experience that a mistake made and shared leads to shared learning. This can be promoted by introducing two awards - one for a great success (e.g. a stuffed fox toy for the whoop) and one for a mistake made (e.g. a stuffed banana toy for the oops) where something has been learned. Only others can nominate you for the biggest success, but only you can nominate yourself for the best mistake. Create a platform, for example every two weeks, where the nomination and awarding of the trophies take place. This way, you playfully learn to report mistakes and share insights.

We have even gotten teams to share their mistakes directly on social media. Successes confirm what you already know; mistakes bring you real new insights when you reflect on them. It's also an insight to know how not to do something. It is important to control the effects of possible mistakes. So don't make any changes to your productive systems with unclear outcome, but rather create test environments. As long as nobody gets hurt, errors are usually worth the investment of the investment of your dues paid. Our tip: It's better to make a mistake and learn something than to do nothing at all.

Do everything at once!

Increase the speed of your teams by letting many people work on many topics at once. Start all projects at the same time so you don't have to prioritize. Many hands make light work!

The number of topics worked on at once equals the factor of time that each topic takes longer than if you would get them done individually in one go without interruption. This means that if you work three projects at the same time, each project will take about three times as long as if you got the three projects done one after the other in a focused way. For this phenomenon, there are simple games to show it takes significantly longer to work on several topics at once, that quality suffers and the use of resources is wasteful. Our brain is not designed to do things at the same time and multi-tasking works poorly with things that require concentration.

1. Create a prioritized list of tasks to be completed. Prioritization

means that there is exactly one priority 1, then one priority 2 and so on. Often, five topics are named as priority 1. This is wrong, not helpful and called grouping.

2. Now work through the topics as an individual or a team according to their priority. Make the list transparent for everyone and in the best case name the reason or value (value in $ is usually most understandable because that's how companies work) of the priority, so that the others can see when their topic is being worked on and why they might have to wait a bit.

3. If there are topics that take a long time or include waiting time try to cut them in a way that makes sense.

4. If you cut topics into subtasks try to get feedback while you are working on other subtasks.

CHAPTER II

Agile Washing

Good software developers are hard to come by. Agility, Scrum and Kanban are popular. The problem: an agile transformation is really exhausting and you have to change a lot. Our tip: Make small changes without much effort and simulate an agile environment. Buy a foosball table, a decent coffee machine, find a mate supplier and the developers will come to you. Now all you have to do is keep them with promises until they are part of your system and don't fight back anymore.

Sticky notes and new names = Scrum!

SCRUM CHECKLIST

- ☐ ~~TO DO List~~ → Sticky Notes
- ☐ ~~Team Meeting~~ → Standup
- ☐ ~~Project Manager~~ → Scrum Master
- ☐ ~~Developers~~ → Dev Ops

Use colorful sticky notes on your windows and have meetings standing up. That's all you need for Scrum. Everything else can stay the same. If someone asks for a more precise implementation of the method, rename meetings and roles. For example, Project Managers are now called Scrum Masters, developers are now DevOps and the weekly reporting is now called Standup.

As soon as you have a hammer, you see nails everywhere. Agile frameworks like Scrum appear and at first glance it looks like Scrum is the solution for all your problems. In our experience, this is rarely the case. Often, there are problems that have to be solved before implementing the Scrum process.

Answer the following questions and make the answers transparent for everyone involved and affected:

- What's your problem?
- Is the nature of your tasks even suitable for using Scrum?
- Are you qualified with regards to different working methods and, therefore, able to make an adequate decision?

If you have simple or complicated, i.e. repetitive tasks that can be solved with an identical or similar approach in case of a new problem, Scrum is not a suitable method. In these cases, it can help to visualize processes with the help of the Kanban method and to measure the lead times in order to then improve the process. However, this requires measuring how long a process takes and where it isn't running smoothly and for which reasons. You must want to do this.

If the tasks are complex and solutions can only be found by trial and error, Scrum can be helpful. In certain periods of time the team works towards a solution. After each iteration it pauses briefly and reflects on the results and the cooperation. For the next iteration, goals and possibly new rules of cooperation are decided upon and the process starts all over again.

It is all right and even beneficial to admit to yourself if you have no idea or you are not able to answer the questions above. If that's the case, let us give you some advice: don't just read a few popular science articles and get going. Scrum is often referred to as a simple method, which in our opinion is not correct as it is used to deal with complexity. Our brain learns through repetition and this is important; again: we need to remember that complexity means that occurring tasks cannot be mastered with an identical solution, but rather that planning, attempting, learning and adapting the procedure are needed steps. Get training for yourself or find qualified help. By qualified help we do not mean that just showing a certification is a guarantee for knowledge and skills. The following questions, for example, can help you with your choice:

- Do you work according to Scrum yourself, even if you are not developing software?
- Which agile methods have you already used yourself?
- Which methods are suitable for what kinds of situations and which advantages and disadvantages do they have?
- How do you measure if the method fits the solution to the problem?

If you want to use Scrum, you have to like transparency. Name a problem, define acceptance criteria, when it is considered solved and work methodically on a solution. If you want to simulate agile methods or Scrum only by renaming existing meetings or roles to make them look modern and interesting for applicants, then this is not a good idea.

Do more, plan less!

Scrum has far too many meetings. During this time, you could also work productively! Combine review, retro and planning and get everything done without preparation in one or two hours. Anything else would not be efficient.

We do not want to repeat the Scrum Guide[1] here, because everything is written down in it and many smart, experienced people have written helpful books and articles. In the beginning, every change is difficult and a frequently asked question is whether the time invested in planning and reflection in Scrum is disproportionate. The answer is: no. The clearer the goal to be achieved (Sprint Vision) and the task packages needed to achieve it (User Stories), the faster a team is during the running time (Sprint), because the prioritized tasks have been understood by everyone in the team and can be worked on. The more focused a team is, the faster it is.

---

[1] https://www.scrumguides.org/

If you start as a team with Scrum, we give you the following recommendations:

- Follow the established ceremonies (Review, Retrospective, Planning, Refinement, Daily) exactly. Perform at least 10 sprints exactly as they are defined. Only then will you as a team be able to decide what is not helpful for you and how you can change it.
- Keep the following order for each sprint change:

  - Do the Review first and invite stakeholders to give feedback and show results.
  - Then, conduct a moderated Retrospective as a team to reflect on the collaboration and define measures for improvement.
  - Include measures from the Retrospective as user stories in your backlog and plan them for the next sprint.

- New things always take longer than expected in the beginning. With time, you will find your routine and you will get faster.
- You will soon have the idea to shorten or cancel ceremonies due to time constraints. Don't, it'll just set you back.
- The clearer and more detailed you document your work, the easier it will be to persevere in stressful situations.

Agile means flexible!

Relativize delays, bad planning and senseless actionism with: We are agile! After all, agility is a synonym for flexible and unplanned.

We can not even count the situations in which plans have been changed spontaneously and without consultation with the justification: "We are agile after all". This is wrong - agile does not mean that everyone does as they please and that things can be changed at any time. For this reason, the word agile is unfortunately already very negatively associated and many people are fed up with it. Often because people use the word without having any knowledge of what agile actually means in terms of working methods.

Working according to agile principles differs significantly from the plan-driven approach. An agile approach is exclusively value-driven and is only suitable for problems in a complex environment, i.e. where the how of solving the problem is still unknown. Agile does not mean unplanned, but rather that regularly a manageable time frame is planned, where changing environmental conditions are incorporated into the planning.

Working according to agile principles means:

- There are clear rules of cooperation.
- Time and budget are fixed.
- The scope to be achieved is variable, so the things that add more value must be completed and delivered before the things that add less value.
- It is clear to everyone involved what is to be achieved and when the goal is reached. The <u>how</u> does not yet have to be clarified in detail.
- The plan for the next weeks, one or two iterations (about two to four weeks per iteration) is very concrete. How do we get closer to the goal?
- If something happens that leads to the current iteration not working on the most important topic, it must be stopped immediately and re-planned. If the project would be finished after this iteration, is the maximum possible value delivered?
- The further one looks into the future, the more vague the plan is. What exactly is done at what point in time and how is it done to get closer to the goal?
- Define key figures for business and technology, which give you information at all times whether the reasonably set target values are reached, undershot or exceeded.

Tip: Solve difficult, hard to estimate, new or completely unclear problems within a topic first, so that the timetable towards the end does not become a gamble.

No Scrum Masters!

Save the money and rather use it to hire developers. Scrum Masters are just annoying. They want to improve, change and make everything measurable. Worst case, the teams are motivated to initiate unpleasant change processes that make management shortcomings transparent. If the demands for Scrum Masters can't be discussed away, appoint project managers, developers or other people who are very busy to Scrum Masters and hope that they don't find the time to do the job well. Full-time Scrum Masters are a first indicator that your classic organization will be turned upside down at some point.

A software development team that is supposed to work according to Scrum is just as ineffective without a Scrum Master as it is without a Product Owner or software developer. Certainly, there are rare exceptions, but the basic rule is: If your teams are to work according to Scrum, they need someone to take care of the technology, someone for the business perspective and someone for the processes. The Scrum Master wears the hat for adherence and continuous improvement of processes and collaboration without disciplinary intervention.

The Scrum Master must lead by conviction, example and experience, not by power. Thea are a serving and not a dominating leader, if one wants to use the term leader at all.

- Per team we recommend 0.6 capacity, i.e. 60% of an individual's working time, as a Scrum Master or more generally as a Process Lead.

- It is helpful if this responsibility rotates within the team and between teams among trained colleague volunteers to keep the fresh wind blowing. This helps to consistently support improvements in collaboration and processes. The regular rotation is important, because even in this role, if you spend too much time in a constant environment, you will quickly become operationally blind. However, since accompanying change is exactly the core of their task, the Scrum Master must not become part of the system.

- The 0.6 is an average value and averages should always be viewed critically. In the beginning, the Scrum Master needs more capacity with a new team, with time, if the team remains stable in this constellation, they need rather less time.

- The basic motivation of a Scrum Master or Process Lead should be to make themselves superfluous. Only if that is the case, the selfless and high aim is to enable the team and to design processes without fearing the loss of one's own tasks afterwards.

- Scrum Masters enable teams to solve their tasks more effectively (do the right things) and more efficiently (do things right).

- The Scrum Master is not there to take over tasks directly and compensate for missing resources or competences. They are there to bring the team into a mode in which the team reaches a constant, healthy speed that it can keep up indefinitely.

- The goal of the Scrum Master is not primarily to increase the productivity of the team but rather to minimize waste.

Every team has the ability to solve a specific problem and achieve a specific goal. The task of the Scrum Master is to uncover these abilities. A nice metaphor is Michelangelo's answer to the question how he was able to create such an incredibly beautiful and precise statue. The question referred to the over five meter high sculpture of David made from a single block of marble. Michelangelo said that David was stuck in the marble block from the beginning. He had only removed what was not David.

The Scrum Master role is often given too little importance. It is only partially filled, not at all or with insufficiently trained people. This is mostly explained with high costs. It is a simple calculation. Assume that a Scrum Master causes similar costs as the other team members. In a team with eight people they only have to make the team 12.5% more effective to amortize their costs. Competent Scrum Masters achieve much more and this does not take into account the influence on the team's environment.

Status reports are called Daily!

Make your teams give you weekly or better daily status reports of their tasks, then explain in as much detail as possible how you want them to fulfil these tasks and what else they should do. Make everyone else stand during these meetings. You may sit on the table or lean against something. Of course, you don't have to tell anyone what you are doing. You can call it a Daily or a Standup.

We encounter many misunderstandings about the Daily or Standup. In our perception, the threshold to introduce a Daily is low as the requirements described here seem easy to understand and realize: have a standing appointment. People like to drop the "daily" requirement under the table, as well as the time frame of maximum 15 minutes or the necessity to be prepared.

- The Daily is a chance for the team to coordinate where they stand in terms of achieving the set (sprint) goal. Guests can attend the Daily in silence and without attracting attention.
- The Product Owner takes part in the Daily to be informed and up to date.
- For young teams, the Scrum Master (Process Lead) moderates the Daily if necessary, ensures that the rules are followed, espe-

cially the time frame. Experienced teams need this less and less.

- Focus and discipline reign in the Daily. Anything distracting is left out. Anything that doesn't affect the team has no relevance in the Daily.

- Detailed clarification talks, questions of principle and discussions must take place outside the Daily.

- Only one person speaks at a time - an object (ball, stuffed animal, pencil) can be passed around to help. Only the person holding the object may speak.

- If points are raised that hinder or even block the team, so-called impediments, the Scrum Master picks them up and resolves them as quickly as possible. The elimination of disturbances, no matter what kind, has the highest priority for the Scrum Master.

- It is helpful to introduce an impediment backlog, to prioritize the impediments and visualize them according to the Kanban method and to make it accessible to everybody. This way, it is transparent what status an impediment is in and when a solution can be expected.

- In the Daily, managers or other people do not give status reports. Numbers or the status of individual tasks can be looked up by management itself in the tool used and maintained by the team. The team sees itself as a broadcaster and therefore has transparent work and documentation locations accessible to everyone, so that no one is dependent on personal information.

- Everybody comes prepared for the Daily! Example: With eight people in a team, each person has about 1.5 minutes. The risk of forgetting something is too high to be unprepared, because only in these 1.5 minutes you have the team's attention. Anything relevant that you don't say in these 1.5 minutes weakens your team in reaching the goal or leads to waste of resources.

Imagine the scenario of a jailbreak for the course of the Daily. The team has only 15 minutes a day in the morning during the yard outing to have a clandestine discussion on who will continue doing what during the day and how to reach the common goal. There is no time for unnecessary debauchery. It must be absolutely clear to everyone who does what by tomorrow in order to get ahead and not get caught.

CHAPTER III

Human Resources and Attitude

As a good HR manager, your job is to tell the applicants everything they want to hear. By the time they realize you have tricked them, they may already be part of the system. Then it's time to nip fresh air and development in the bud and leave unwilling zombie working machines who will only do what your company wants until they self-destruct.

Employer Branding is the be-all and end-all!

Invest in employer branding and tell your applicants about your supposed startup mentality and tell them whatever they want to hear to get them on board. Ignore the fact that most people quit within the first few days after encountering what reality actually looks like after being hired. If it takes a month to order a pen or the CFO releases 100 € amounts, you simply justify that as "historically grown" processes.

Employer branding has become one of our most hated terms. You either are a cool employer and take your duty of care seriously or you're not. Expensive video productions, social media appearances, exhibition stands, campaigns and recruiting events disguised as initiatives or conferences are of no use if they convey a false company image. In our experience, the image of the employer drawn in the context of employer branding is often what the employer would like to be and not what it really is. Are you from the HR department and did we step on some toes with the previous statements? Then answer the following three exemplary questions critically:

1. Have you also included employees who are critical of the company in employer branding measures?
2. Have you named things that don't work so well?
3. Do you evaluate the value the employer branding measures add?

If you can honestly answer just these three questions positively, your company has done a lot differently from what we have encountered. There are now enough portals where employees or applicants can share their experiences. The shiny first impression will soon be forgotten if the onboarding doesn't work smoothly, if no hardware is ordered, if there is no workstation available or if the promises made during the application process don't come true. Nothing is more credible and has proven to be economically more profitable in terms of satisfaction, seniority and no disappointed expectations than winning new colleagues based on employees-recruit-employees campaigns.

- Develop an employees-recruit-employees concept together with existing employees.
- Invest the employer branding budget supposed to be used for fancy marketing campaigns in the working environment and your employees. If they enjoy working for you, they will spread the word that you are a good employer and recommend you to future employees.
- Carry out regular surveys among the existing workforce on working conditions and make the unvarnished results transparent. Afterwards, derive measures and implement them consistently.

- There is no market balance when it comes to skilled labor. There is way more demand than applicants. Every lie, whether directly or indirectly mediated, is a loan that your company will eventually pay for. When word gets around that many disappointments await behind the beautiful facade, only skilled workers who have not found anything elsewhere will come to you.

Pressure increases performance!

Pay people in positions with customer contact poorly and place only a few people in such positions so they are well utilized and no idle time occurs. Where there is a queue on one side, there is a fully occupied position on the other side. And pressure increases performance - after all, that's true of combustion engines.

Employees in customer service or internal support functions such as IT, the post office and the canteen are the first point of contact, which people often turn to with problems. This is a decisive factor for both customer and employee satisfaction. This requires a wide range of skills, such as a broad knowledge of the company, its processes and contact persons, problem-solving skills, communication skills, possibly in several languages, and de-escalation skills.

These positions are often difficult to fill and are characterized by frequent fluctuation. On closer inspection, it quickly becomes clear why: low salaries, working in shifts, complicated tool landscape, performance measured on closed (rejected) rather than solved requests, and little recognition are common. The value of

43

these jobs for the company as a whole can be seen in the number of contacts and dependent turnover with customers, as well as quick reaction and helpful solutions for saving work time and work ability of employees. Nevertheless, precisely these interfaces are very often filled with completely unsuitable people. Sometimes out of convenience ("I've been doing this for 20 years.") or for budget reasons. The results are collapsing bridges, data scandals, incorrectly delivered mail, dissatisfied employees and dissatisfied customers.

- Create an overview of which positions in your company are relevant for this.
- Choose title and payment according to this value. Note: Customers and employees are multipliers for negative rather than positive things.
- Design the working conditions together with the employees deployed here.
- Pay attention to appreciation and health.
- As part of initial training and as a recurring awareness-raising measure, make temporary employment in such positions compulsory for all employees.
- For true customer orientation, every employee should regularly be present as a listener or helper when interacting with customers.

Customers and employees participate 100% in the value creation of your company. Dealing with them has a perspective effect on the future of your company.

Build your own office supplies storage!

Do you never find a pad, ballpoint pen or highlighter in the office supplies storage when you need it? Or do your colleagues annoy you with requests for sticky notes because you are the person who orders them and has to deal with internal purchasing and the order platform in the 90s look?

As soon as the next delivery arrives, better take a few more things with you and store them in your lockable roll-away container - just for you or at most your favorite colleagues.

If the value in euros of all private office supplies storages is added up, many companies will have a tidy sum. We experience that most of them are dissatisfied with this mode - consumers like orderers, internal purchasing and the person releasing the orders. The trouble is that it blocks the productivity of people who need something. When a department moves or someone leaves the company, many office supplies that are found have passed their expiry date and are thrown away.

Waste of time, productivity and office supplies can easily be reduced. Organize the office supplies storage as a Kanban shelf. This has been used in production for many years and storage is based on the first-in-first-out principle. What helps in the control of production processes also helps to ensure that you always have envelopes, transparent film, printer paper, pens, adhesive labels, chargers and whatever other office supplies you use in stock, while keeping tied costs as low as possible.

Take a shelf and collect all the office supplies of your department, dissolve all private storages and storages 2 to 25. We are always amazed at how much stuff can be found. Sort the material by type in a compartment or in a box - depending on the type and size of the shelves. Paper clips to paper clips, staples to staples and so on.

Order Kanban document holders or something similar to match the size of the boxes or width of the shelves. It is important that you can insert small cards at a defined place. For each item you need three cards in the colors green, red and yellow. On each of these slips of paper you write down:

- the article with a clear description, e.g. whiteboard marker black, refillable,
- the minimum quantity, e.g. 5 pieces,
- the order quantity, e.g. 20 pieces, and
- additional information on the back.

The minimum quantity indicates when the reorder process is triggered. The order quantity specifies how much is reordered. In large systems, it is useful to write the supplier, order number(s) and contact person(s) on the back of the order.

Depending on the procurement process and the frequency of order cycles, you now determine the quantity of each item that must not be undercut (minimum quantity), e.g. 10 black ballpoint pens, and the order quantity, e.g. 30 pieces. Take into account the frequency of use and the duration of an order.

The three colors of the slips of paper that are inserted one after the other in the Kanban document holder have the following meaning:

- Green = Above the critical order quantity, everything in the literally green area.
- Red = Below critical order quantity, please order.
- Yellow = Order has been placed and we are waiting for delivery.

Let's stick to the ballpoint pen example: In a compartment there are black ballpoint pens - the green card is in front. If someone takes the 10th ballpoint pen out of the package, the minimum quantity of 10 is undercut, there are only 9 ballpoint pens left. They now put the red card in front. Regularly, for example once a week, the person who places the orders for the office supplies storage goes to the shelf, takes all the red cards out and puts the yellow cards in front. They make the necessary orders - e.g. meaning 30 ballpoint pens are ordered. When the orders are placed, the red cards are put back into the document holders at the back, the yellow cards remain at the front. Only when the office supplies have arrived and been sorted are the green cards put back in the front. The red and yellow cards remain behind them.

This way, only what has just been used is ordered, and everyone involved can see the current status of the item. Furthermore, the presence of the red card indicates whether the order has already been placed or not.

The initial effort may seem time-consuming. However, once installed, the Kanban office supplies storage is a sure-fire success after an initial strict education, demonstration and explanation period. Kanban promotes mindfulness and self-organization. It is also a good way to experience that Kanban is a method for process optimization, improves throughput and eliminates waiting times. Once this principle is understood, it can be used anywhere in the company. In the kitchen, for cleaning products, for light bulbs and of course, for production equipment. Wherever employees see these cards, they know how the process works.

Set up as many obstacles as you can!

In your business, you are the lawmaker. If something does work or is possible without you wanting it to, think of obstacles, build barriers and justify them with privacy, compliance or security.

Every company has its own culture that has developed over time. The corporate culture is influenced by internal and external factors. Internal factors are, for example, the composition of the workforce, company processes or the behavior of managers. External factors are the labor market, politics or the location of a company or branch. We have experienced in a lot of companies that over time, there is a change from the we to the I, from our problem-solving culture to my problem-solving culture, from self-organization to bureaucracy.

In self-organization, everyone is responsible for the consequences of their actions. In bureaucracy, a person is separated from the consequences of their actions. Doing nothing is actually also an action. We have experienced situations so severely restricted by regulations that the processes only served to comply with rules and the solution of the original problem was only secondary. We have seen employees who were not allowed to access their own personnel files for data protection reasons. We have seen computers that, for compliance and security reasons, were so limited in their function they could no longer be used to perform their actual tasks. Imagine a watchmaker who has to wear huge, thick gloves for health and safety reasons, or a delivery service whose vehicles have all their wheels removed and their bodies all bolted to the floor, because if they could move, they could be used to move company data. It is absurd, but many companies invest 120 € in personnel costs (because the process is so long and complicated) to order 10 pens worth 5 €. The whole thing takes another 14 days. The value of personnel costs due to a high investment of time because of a complicated process exceeds the benefit many times over. No value is created for the customer or the company either by the deed or in the time spent on it. There are many companies that have made compliance the sole reason for their existence by setting absurd rules for themselves. Helpful solutions are the following:

- Have a close look at your processes and regularly check that they are fulfilling their primary function.
- Use your own processes.
- Use your IT data and build automated key figures in all processes.
- Establish thresholds to check processes.
- Visualize key figures - for everyone.
- If employees bypass processes, there are reasons for it, find them and improve the process.

- Make all processes transparent - for everyone. Start with the process for change.

- Every process has exactly one person responsible, who, if possible, is often involved in the process.

- Change your perspective, try to do other people's jobs.

- Offer employees the opportunity to swap tasks (temporarily) and use the insights to improve something.

- Establish feedback loops (e.g. moderated, regular Retrospectives).

- Try to create an environment in which processes can be understood with common sense and without outside help (Example: Revolving door. Nobody needs instructions to use a revolving door).

CHAPTER IV

Software Developers and IT

As a software developer or IT employee, you have a special status. You can do whatever you want, you just have to justify it in a complicated enough way. In the end, nobody understands anything anyway. You do what you enjoy and what you think is right, everything else doesn't work for some reason.

Make maintenance work noticeable!

Always schedule updates, backups with large amounts of data and hardware changes during the working hours of as many users as possible - preferably unannounced. People should be able to notice you are working. An untested, two-hour update of the calendar and e-mail system on a Tuesday at 10:00 am is perfectly fine.

The smooth and intuitive use of IT and IT infrastructure is the key to determining whether a company will survive in the future or not. Strongly abstracted (and very simplified), we observe three large dimensions:

The management: Here we notice that IT requires more and more costs and personnel. However, direct profits from IT are rather difficult to determine, if at all. What does the IT department actually do all day long?

The users: They always want everything to work. They rarely want to give useful feedback because it's too much work. In the canteen, they prefer to gossip about IT rather than clearly expressing expectations. What does the IT department actually do all day long?

The IT department: They feel left alone by the management, have to justify themselves for every euro spent and are annoyed by the stupid users who break their systems and don't understand anything. Most employees have a full overtime account, but nobody appreciates their work.

But what now?

- One way to alleviate this situation is full transparency of IT: Show which projects you are working on, what they cost and which improvements they bring.
- Make your future tasks (backlog) visible for everyone and explain the prioritization. This way, everybody knows where their problem stands on your list and that it has not been forgotten. They can also see why it has not been solved yet, because there are so many other things to do that are considered more important.
- When it comes to the IT department itself, it helps to concentrate on the problems that are currently ranked the highest priorities and not those where someone is screaming particularly loudly.

The best IT administrator is the one you don't see or have to call because updates and changes are not subject to restrictions. In case of updates or changes not possible without user restrictions, please announce them ahead of time and explain why they are necessary. This helps with acceptance. Relationships with management and users will then automatically improve, and at best, your example of transparency will rub off on others. When people in the IT department are aware of their responsibility for the impact on customer and employee satisfaction and the importance for the company's figures, a lot can be achieved. And one thing is clear: No company can be successful without superstars in the IT department.

You determine the choice of hardware!

As an IT professional, you determine what hardware the rank and file has to use. If the small woman in the field complains about the weight of her notebook, she should go to the gym. And why should anyone get an additional travel charger? Is it too much to ask for them to crawl under their desk twice a day?

As different as people are, so are their preferences when it comes to hardware. For cost reasons and the possibility of volume discounts, the central IT department often selects models that seem suitable for them. For most employees, however, they are not.

- Let your employees choose which hardware they want to use. The cost of heterogeneity will pay off, because people are more productive when they work with devices they like.
- Empower rather than patronize - empower employees to use technology rather than forbid them to do things.
- Train your employees in media literacy so they are less vulnerable to spam, scam, viruses, worms, and Trojans.

- Include employees supposed to use beamers, video conferencing systems or printers in the selection process of the devices.
- Don't make cost and efficiency the sole criteria for hardware choices.

Companies that dictate an exchangeable standard workplace to all employees and demand that they be self-organized, motivated and creative will not attract capable employees in the future. All generations since the 1990s have grown up with information technology. These digital natives now have their infrastructure and tools imposed on them by digital immigrants. It's as if a native Spanish speaker was told how to speak from now on by a German who has been learning Spanish grammar rules by heart for five years. Have confidence in the competence of your employees and offer them choices, help and solutions, but don't be dogmatic. The goal is for everyone to always learn something new.

Document nothing!

Documentation is pointless. Good code and good software don't need documentation. It's a waste of time, everything changes all the time anyway, and its better to have no documentation at all than to have outdated documentation.

If this belief is rooted and has become a collective attitude, action will confirm this very fact: Documentation is either completely missing or it's not useful because it's bad or incomplete. This way, it only creates more work and doesn't benefit anyone, and therefore, the effort is high while the benefit is low.

- The only thing that helps in these kinds of situations is to rethink consistently and define documentation as an integral part of systems or features, which must be available at the time of acceptance and is a criterion for terminating the commissioning process if it's not available or not sufficiently available.

- To establish this, documentation can be part of a Definition of Done, the criteria that must be met for a task, feature or system to be considered complete and delivered to the customer.

The Manifesto for Agile Software Development states: "Functioning software more than comprehensive documentation". This sentence (without a verb) is often taken out of context and in people's minds it's left: Better to add a new function than to document another one. This is not only strongly misinterpreted but also negligent. This statement is not only about documentation in the sense of operating instructions. Software and IT systems are becoming increasingly complex. A lack of documentation leads to processes for quality assurance, for example, no longer being (able to be) carried out. Let's assume a company has to plan how certain systems are to be maintained in the future. However, if some of these systems are not documented anywhere, they will not be included in regular maintenance. Whether in cases of illness, holidays or unforeseen situations, missing or inadequate documentation is a major reason for blocked productivity. Lack of documentation is a risk credit with regards to which you don't know how expensive it will be once you have to pay for it. There are quite a few companies operating software and IT systems in strategically important positions without having any knowledge on them, because all consultants, service providers and employees who have worked with them at some point are no longer available and reengineering would be incredibly costly. Some of them no longer even dare to update or restart machines and expose themselves, their employees and customers to unnecessary and incalculable risks. The rule that should be derived from the above sentence from the Agile Manifesto is: Don't start developing a new feature before the old one is well documented.

Don't hoard hardware!

The IT department is not a computer shop. Toner for the printers is only ordered when it's completely used up. Notebooks, cables, keyboards, track pads and mice are not stored - this is far too expensive. If users lose or break something, they have to wait.

This procedure is very common and very expensive. The longer the discussion time about the need, the time to approve the order or the wait for the spare part is, the longer the employee cannot work and frustration increases enormously whereas productivity decreases continuously.

- Know the most commonly used devices because you have statistics about the issued devices and evaluate them.
- Always have the most common replacement equipment and parts in stock in a certain quantity - according to the amount of wear and tear, duration of the order process and number of employees.

- Make access to spare parts as easy as possible for the user. Remember: They just want to do their job and also don't feel like discussing with you and spending time on it.
- Set up a Kanban storage for the most frequently needed items.

The effort and costs of a well thought-out management of production resources are much less expensive than the loss of productivity if you don't have this kind of management of production resources.

Never test anything!

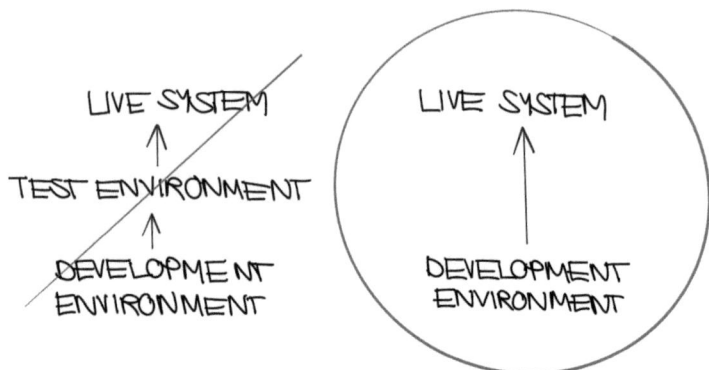

Your code is secure and side effects are under control. Implement changes directly into the live system. This is cost-saving and fast. Test environments, quality assurance and staging are for hipsters who have too much time and money.

Although reports of (customer) data loss are increasingly appearing in the media, the subject of testing is still being treated badly. Untested software is regularly let loose on customers. Devices fail in their core functions during commissioning. Processes don't come close to achieving the desired result. The effects of errors in productive operation usually cannot be estimated. The effort required for testing, however, is calculable. So why exchange something calculable for something incalculable? Tests can be automated and must be part of every process. Not only must the actual function be tested, but the new function must also be tested in its ultimate environment. These so-called integration tests are not only important for software. Just because a method or solution has been successfully implemented somewhere, it does not mean that it can be successfully implemented in another environment unchanged and untested. What is important when testing is that the expected result is defined beforehand and that the test is not adapted to the result.

Since the topic is sufficiently described in the net and in the expert literature, we only give this one tip:

- Always test, test, test.

Testing is always cheaper than sweeping up the broken pieces afterwards. You can also learn from failed tests. Learning costs, which you have to pay because you deliberately refrained from testing, are unnecessary.

CHAPTER V

Product Development and Customer Contact

Just say the customer is king and build your products and processes the way you like them. You decide what your customer likes and what they want to pay for. They should be grateful when they can pay for it and spend their lifetime testing your new ideas. But always do it nice and slow and in homeopathic dosages, so customers don't get stupid thoughts and make absurd demands, for example a balanced price-performance ratio or the implementation of advertised functions. As for customer support, the golden rule applies: Absence makes the heart grow fonder.

Don't have visions!

Don't have a vision for your company or product, let alone a clear or desirable one. If it's not clear where the journey is going, you can make everything seem like a success and nobody can criticize you.

We are often asked to explain the concepts of "vision" and "mission" in our own words as well as the difference between these two. Hence the following introduction: In order to enable people to make decisions on their own authority in the sense of a common cause, they must know what the common cause is - and actively choose to support it. The vision focuses on tomorrow and makes it clear what the product or company wants to be like in the future. It is formulated in a measurable way so that it's clear to everyone whether they are getting closer to the envisioned state or even moving further away from it as a result of certain actions. The vision thus sets the direction. The mission breaks the vision down into today and everything that the company and the employees have to do today in order to achieve the vision tomorrow - formulated in a measurable way to make sure it is possible to review at any given time, whether we are heading towards it with our decisions and actions or whether we are moving further away from it.

Vision and mission are fundamental at the overall company level as well as for each department, product and team or work group - they pay off. These tips may sound simple, but we often experience that implementation is a major challenge:

- Define a measurably formulated vision and mission.
- Define the framework and the interaction of vision and mission, for example by using annual or quarterly targets. Agree on a clear scope of action with teams and individuals so they can achieve the goals in a self-organized manner.
- Make this visible to all and transparent in writing.
- Give employees the opportunity to participate in shaping the mission or at least to ask questions.

Good visions sound impossible, crazy and unrealistic the first time they are expressed. They are a definite blueprint for the future. Goals become more understandable to everyone when the "why?" is explained. From know-how to know-why. What does it mean to become better? Why do we want to increase revenue?

Not having goals is not an option. Sure, if you don't have goals or plans you can't be disappointed. But you won't achieve any goals which currently seem utopian to you, either.

Actionism, now!

Implement your first idea or someone else's idea directly without understanding the problem. You need to act, act, act. Never test several ideas and don't make decisions based on (measurable) criteria. Your gut feeling will guide you and you should always listen to it!

An important, necessary feature in management is the ability to decide whether to react in firefighter mode or to try and understand the situation calmly and then make a value-driven decision. In rare cases, it's necessary to make a decision immediately and without further information. Not acting is also a decision, by the way. And even if there is a real fire, you should not make any daring attempts to put it out, but rather keep calm and call the firefighters. Staying calm and calling in someone who is an expert on the subject is also a sensible way to deal with critical situations.

The proverbial gut decisions are deceiving because they are often generalized or confused with chance. First of all, gut decisions do not come from the stomach, but from the brain. We rely on our experiences for such decisions. In mechanical engineering, human resources, medicine or IT, this is similar to driving a car. The longer you practice a discipline, the better your decisions in this area, even in situations that are new to you. In a dangerous situation, our brain takes all stored information on the appropriate topic and calculates the variant with the highest probability of survival in a fraction of a second. Someone who has worked in an industry for 30 years and is mentally healthy will normally make a better decision in unknown emergency situations than someone who has five years of experience. Once you made a good decision in an unknown situation in your field, consider the following two tips:

1. Your experience is not transferable to other areas of expertise.
2. Do not confuse success with coincidence.

Try to decide based on rational means as much as possible - also when choosing your advisors. Think about what qualities the person you're looking for should have before making a decision. Make a list with a simple scale, have conversations in which you learn the qualities directly or indirectly, and then decide according to the result of your list, not sympathy. Sympathy is the sum of all similarities. This means if you're sitting on a mistake, you will find a person reinforcing that mistake more sympathetic or competent than a person arguing against that mistake. If you then commission based on sympathy, there are already two people subject to error and you take away the opportunity to get closer to the problem.

Review your decisions to find out if they were good decisions to challenge your decision-making process. To do this, you must first define what is good for you when you look at the outcome in a year or ten years. Any decision you make without precise background information, you can rationally weigh up, is at high risk of being the wrong decision. The further away the topic is from your area of expertise, the higher the risk. Therefore, try to quickly obtain information that will help you make a decision. This doesn't mean that you can take a long time or postpone decisions. If there are no lives or extremely high sums at stake, it's better to make the wrong decision (and correct it when you notice it) than not to make a decision at all. Learning from a wrong decision is often more valuable than the supposed loss due to this wrong decision. Our personal clues, which allow a short delay, are human life, serious illness or damage greater than 100.000 € being at stake. Otherwise, we decide on the basis of the available data and check the results in short iterations. If it turns out that a decision doesn't lead to the desired result, we change it. And this is what makes the difference to colloquial actionism, which assumes aimless, conceptless or unreflected action.

If you work on or in an environment with self-organized teams, there are fewer decisions made by individuals, because decisions are usually made by teams in certain cycles. This is a good way to prevent actionism. However, the environment and especially superiors have to get involved and respect the decisions of the teams.

Install prerecorded phone announcements!

Replace your hotline with an announcement that there is currently an increased call volume and all employees are in conversation. Then disconnect the connection. The customer will find other ways to get rid of their problem.

And under no circumstances allow contact by e-mail, at most via a chat or a message function in the customer account, which can be "not working" if necessary.

Nobody wants problems. If any do occur, it's in the interest of all parties to solve them quickly and easily. To do this, it's helpful to put yourself in the position of the person concerned and ask yourself:

- Is it possible to get information to solve the problem?
- If so, is the information to be found (simply) described in such a way that even someone from outside the profession could use this manual to solve the problem?
- Can the information be found by non-IT experts at all?
- If the problem itself cannot be solved, what possibilities are there to reach someone who can help?
- How long does it take to solve a problem?

Instructions are often written in a way that the person writing them or someone with expertise can understand the text - but not a person who is, for example, a user and not a developer of a service.

- It's usually helpful to provide a portal with information for self-service and to inform all employees or customers about its existence, preferably with a short introduction - in text, video and image form.
- A customer account with a high level of self-service (for customers and employees) can be restricted or extended in its rights as required. This can save a lot of work for the people helping.

When all the possibilities are there and yet, no solution to the problem can be found by the person concerned themself, it's important to offer fast, direct help:

- Provide different possibilities to get in contact and make your processes of handling transparent.
- Measure at what times there is a particularly high level of need for help and adjust your staff planning accordingly.
- Treat your users like customers. Ask for feedback regularly and check if your offered help options work and are usable.

75

#teamagile

https://www.teamagile.org/